DR. DAN

Dear Alvin + Kate,

Stir up your

gifts!

II Timothy 1:6,7

Love in Christ,

Dr. Dan Olawa

ISBN 978-1514782330

www.isonrise.org

CONTENTS

INTRODUCTION
THE SOURCE OF ALL SOURCES

WHERE DO I FIT?

Study and write, study and write, study and write... hand in your work and get a grade, but sometimes all that studying just doesn't seem to mean anything in a *who-needs-this-stuff-for-real-life* kind of way. So, how does information and knowledge apply to today, to me, to my destiny, my future? If it doesn't apply... *what's the point?*

Teachers and professors would argue that all knowledge is beneficial. That it may not teach you something you can use for a practical life application, but it WILL teach you how to think for yourself, how to interact and reason. THAT everyone can use, for sure. What if you *could* learn something real and practical, something you could *instantly* touch... something so intimately personal that it's pointing straight at YOU? What if discovering how God made you would help you understand WHY He made you and WHAT on earth you are here to do? What if you could learn something that would DEFINE your life, give you meaning and purpose? *Interested?*

Everyone Gets a Gift From God.

Did you get that? *Everyone!* Does that mean people who don't acknowledge or relate to God still get gifts? Yes, and some people can get more than one and even many gifts, but for now we are dealing with the gifts of God as they relate to the Body of Christ. Each single gift is so personal and useful that no one is left out.

1 Corinthians 12:1, *"Now concerning spiritual gifts, brethren, I do not want you to be ignorant."*

The Person of the Holy Spirit

The Holy Spirit:

- Is THE Source

- Continually points us to Jesus

- Teaches – John 14:26, *"But the Helper, the Holy Spirit, whom the Father will send in My name, He will teach you all things, and bring to your remembrance all things that I said to you."*

- Bears witness to Jesus Christ – John 15:26, *"But when the Helper comes, whom I shall send to you from the Father, the Spirit of truth who proceeds from the Father, He will testify of Me."*

- Can be lied to – Acts 5:3, *"But Peter said, 'Ananias, why has Satan filled your heart to lie to the Holy Spirit and keep back part of the price of the land for yourself?'"*

- Intercedes according to the mind and will of God – Romans 8:26-28, *"Likewise the Spirit also helps in our weaknesses. For we do not know what we should pray for as we ought, but the Spirit Himself makes intercession for us with groanings which cannot be uttered. Now He who searches the hearts knows what the mind of the Spirit is, because He makes intercession for the saints according to the will of God."*

- Wills – 1 Corinthians 12:11, *"But one and the same Spirit works all these things, distributing to each one individually as He wills."*

- Feels – Ephesians 4:30, *"And do not grieve the Holy Spirit of God, by whom you were sealed for the day of redemption."*

- Speaks – Revelation 2:7, *"He who has an ear, let him hear what the Spirit says to the churches. To him who overcomes I will give to eat from the tree of life, which is in the midst of the Paradise of God."*

- Displays personality – mind, will and emotions

- Is the THIRD PERSON of the Trinity

- Is THE wooer of God

- Fills us or indwells us (walk in, live in, love through and commune with the Holy Spirit)

Your Gift Comes From the Holy Spirit.

Gifts from the Holy Spirit are separated into three categories according to the Bible. Let's not be ignorant! Check it out.

Motivational Gifts (Romans 12:3-9)

_____

_____

_____

_____

_____

_____

_____

Ministry Gifts (1 Corinthians 12:27-31; Ephesians 4)

_____

_____

_____

_____

Manifestational Gifts (1 Corinthians 12:7-11)

_____

_____

_____

_____

_____

_____

_____

_____

If you exercise your motivational gift through your ministry gift, the Holy Spirit manifests, touching and blessing people.

Why *does* God give gifts to mankind? How do we minister to people's needs and help others discover the personal will of God for their lives?

Upon examination of the variety of Holy Spirit gifts listed in the Bible and described in the chapters that follow, please note that these gifts are/were not principally intended for the benefit of the one who has (possesses) the gift! In these examples and definitions the gifts are essentially used for the Body of Christ as a whole, and for individual persons in the Body of Christ. Think about that and write down your comments on how specific gifts can affect others.

_____

_____

_____

_____

_____

_____

_____

_____

_____

_____

_____

_____

_____

_____

_____

_____

_____

_____

_____

Motivational (charismation)

God puts inward motivation inside you in order to show His love. 1 Corinthians 12:4, *"There are diversities of gifts, but the same Spirit."*

Ministry (diakonion)

The Christian service gifts are used to exercise one's motivation. 1 Corinthians 12:5, *"There are differences of ministries, but the same Lord."*

Manifestational (enegema phanerosis)

The manifestations of the Spirit are concrete evidence to help those who are receiving ministry. 1 Corinthians 12:6, *"And there are diversities of activities, but it is the same God who works all in all."*

In this study we will look at the Person of the Holy Spirit, the source of your gift(s).

CHAPTER ONE
THE IRREVOCABLE GIFTS OF THE HOLY SPIRIT

Want to Know God's Will in Your Life?

Get to Know Your Gift(s).

Romans 11:29, *"For the gifts and the calling of God are irrevocable."*

Romans 12:1-2, *"I beseech you therefore, brethren, by the mercies of God, that you present your bodies a living sacrifice, holy, acceptable to God, which is your reasonable service. And do not be conformed to this world, but be transformed by the renewing of your mind, that you may prove what is that good and acceptable and perfect will of God."*

Romans 12:3, *"For I say, through the grace given to me, to everyone who is among you, not to think of himself more highly than he ought to think, but to think soberly, as God has dealt to each one a measure of faith."*

<u>Negative</u> – Don't think higher of yourself than you should (also don't be self-abasing, but humble).

<u>Positive</u> – We all receive a measure of faith. We are all different and completely unique.

Romans 12:4, *"For as we have many members in one body, but all the members do not have the same function."*

The Body of Christ has many members, all unique!

Office – *praxis* – means "practice", that is concretely an act; by extension, a function of a deed, office, work.

One Body

Romans 12:5-6, *"So we, being many, are one body in Christ, and individually members of one another. Having then gifts differing according to the grace that is given to us, let us use them: if prophecy, let us prophesy in proportion to our faith."*

We are *designed* to do our part (v.5).

We have gifts differing according to the grace given us (v.6).

1 Corinthians 12:18, *"…God has set the members, each one of them, in the body just as He pleased."*

Discerning God's Will – Knowing Our Gifts

We see in these verses that one way of discerning or knowing God's will is by knowing our giftedness and calling.

What is a Spiritual Gift?

"A spiritual gift is a supernatural attribute given by the Holy Spirit to every member of the Body of Christ, according to God's grace, for use within the context of the Body."[1]

- Every Christian has a gift!

- Many Christians are multi-gifted.

- YOUR calling and your gift go hand in hand!

A person's calling and his or her spiritual gifts are very closely related.

1 Peter 4:10, *"As each one has received a gift, minister it to one another, as good stewards of the manifold grace of God."*

Greek Definitions for "Spiritual Gift"

The common Greek word for "spiritual gift" is *charisma*. The plural is *charismata*. The word comes from *charis*, which in Greek means *"grace."*

"Spiritual gift" is *pneumatikos* – G4151. From the word *pneuma*, *pnyoo'-mah*; a current of air, *i.e.*, breath (blast) or a breeze; by anal. or fig. a spirit, *i.e.*, (human) the rational soul, (by impl.) vital principle, as used in 1 Corinthians 12:1, *"Now concerning spiritual gifts...."*[2]

Greek Definition of "Gift"

A general word for gift is *doma* – meaning "a present or gift."

Benefits of Spiritual Gifts

- Get to know yourself

- You know what you are about

- You know what you are, so far

Who Benefits?

Your gift benefits the Body of Christ. Your gift helps the body mature. Ephesians 4:13-14, *"Till we all come to the unity of the faith and of the knowledge of the Son of God, to a perfect man, to the measure of the stature of the fullness of Christ; that we should no longer be children, tossed to and fro and carried about with every wind of doctrine, by the trickery of men, in the cunning craftiness of deceitful plotting."*

The Result

Use of your spiritual gift brings glory to God. 1 Peter 4:10-11, *"As each one has received a gift, minister it to one another, as good stewards of the manifold grace of God. If anyone speaks, let him speak as the oracles of God. If anyone ministers, let him do it as with the ability which God supplies, that in all things God may be glorified through Jesus Christ, to whom belong the glory and the dominion forever and ever Amen."*

Dangers and Abuses of the Gifts

- Watch out for gift exaltation *i.e.*, putting one gift above the others.

- Remember that ALL gifts are important.

- Be careful of gift projection.

- "Everyone should be like me." *NOT!*

Guilt

- Don't wallow in your own guilt.

- Don't guilt-trip others.

- Be who you are.

- 1 Corinthians 12:11 – *"The Holy Spirit gives the gifts as He wills."*

- Love is the key.

1 Corinthians 13 – Love, love, love…did I say, *"LOVE?"*

Discover Your Gifts

Start! You must be a Christian for the gift to make sense. Study what the Bible says about the gifts. Launch out by asking your spiritual leaders or mentors where you can use your gifts. Pray.

Try Different Things

Experiment.

What Do You Like to Do?

Evaluate things you are NOW doing effectively.

Expect the Body of Christ to Confirm It

Listen to the Lord and His confirmation through others!

Personal Application:

Pray! Launch Out! Develop your gifts!

Defining Gifts: THREE Things Gifts Are Not

1. Spiritual gifts are not natural talents

   - We are all created in the image of God.

   - Putting on a muffler may be a natural ability.

   - We hear of "charismatic" leaders. Some have a charismatic personality which is a natural talent not a spiritual gift.

   - Spiritual gifts are for believers.

   - Sometimes God uses a natural talent. John Wimber had a natural ability as a salesman and God used that in his evangelism gift. But not all salesmen are evangelists.

2. Spiritual gifts are not the fruit of the Spirit

   - The fruit of the Spirit is the normal outcome of Christian growth, maturity, etc. All of us have a responsibility to progressively develop the fruit of the Spirit.

- The gifts of the Spirit and the fruit of the Spirit are designed to work hand in hand. Gifts without the fruit of the Spirit are worthless.

- Gifts are task-oriented. The fruit is God-oriented.

- Every passage on the gifts of the Holy Spirit has something to do with the fruit of the Spirit.

- Love is the central focus through which all the fruit of the Spirit must be displayed. Gifts expressed without love are worthless.

3. Spiritual gifts are not Christian roles

- Many of the gifts are roles in other Christians' lives.

- Prayer, faith, mercy, hospitality, evangelism, etc.

CHAPTER TWO
MOTIVATIONAL GIFTS

WHAT MOVES ME TO ACTION?

Motivational gifts tug on heartstrings and stir up emotion, luring us to action. One or more of these gifts can inspire and prompt its expression in the Body of Christ and out in our communities. Earnestly seek the Lord to identify your own gifts instead of compartmentalizing others.

Let's check out what motivates you and see how some obsessions can be a good thing!

THE GIFT OF SERVING

Read Philippians 2:19-22 and describe what Paul says about Timothy:

_____

_____

_____

_____

_____

The Greek word, *diakonian* means, "ministering." Ministering is another term for serving.

God has given the gift of serving as a supernatural ability to minister to the needs of others. Anyone CAN serve – and should, but those who are servants by gifting in the Body of Christ can quickly identify and anticipate needs with ease. It's like getting your water glass filled at a restaurant before you even ask! It's premium spiritual customer service, in a big way! Whatever available resource is handy will get used to meet needs and assist leadership goals.

Read Luke 22:24-27 and describe your thoughts on the attitude and ultimate goal of a gifted servant.

_____

_____

_____

_____

_____

Serving with joy frees others to do more important things. Give a practical example:

_____

_____

_____

_____

_____

Servant Character Qualities

People with a gift of serving are passionate servers! Highly energetic with extreme attention to details, gifted servants don't hesitate to become involved whenever an opportunity to serve arises.

I am married to Terry, a gifted servant. I have watched her operate for the last 37 years. She enjoys projects, checklists, planning and finishing tasks. Terry is extremely detail-oriented. Her energy to serve completely astounds and tires me out just watching her! She is MOTIVATED to serve! Terry shows her love for God and others through completion of tasks, deeds and hospitality. She rarely forgets even the smallest of details.

Servant Downside

Terry sometimes plans too much to do in a single day and would say I probably don't plan enough! She applies tremendous energy when serving to the point of wearing herself out. Sometimes it is hard for her to say no since she is immediately motivated to meet needs as they arise. Another example is a story about a couple of ladies who were recently asked at the last minute to serve at a wedding. Because of their gifting as servants they already had too much on their plates and should have said no, but you guessed it, they said yes and worked to the point of exhaustion! While laboring, they expressed their annoyances out loud to anyone who would listen. I told them if they wanted to know who they should get upset with they should glance in a mirror. I told them they should have said no to begin with when asked to do the wedding. Servers often wonder why everyone does not serve as they do, with great enthusiasm and passion! The truth is, not everyone has the gift of serving!

Servants need to constantly reassess their priorities and guard their family time and resources. They also need to learn to graciously receive from others.

THE GIFT OF TEACHING

Read Acts 18:24-28, 1 & 2 Timothy and Acts 18:1-3. Then describe Apollos, Timothy and Aquila as teachers:

_____

_____

_____

_____

_____

The Greek word, *didasko* means, "to teach" or to "teach one."

"God has given the gift of teaching as a supernatural ability to communicate information in a way that is easy to grasp. This ability is especially relevant to the health and ministry of the Body of Christ."[3]

Describe your thoughts on the attitude and ultimate goal of the gift of teaching.

_____

_____

_____

_____

_____

Teacher Character Qualities

The gift of teaching is an amazing gift. One of our church staff pastors is Doug Martin. He is a gifted teacher, also coupled with a gift of serving. In my experience, most people are multi-gifted though not even aware of it.

Doug loves to study the scripture, words, biblical characters and enjoys teaching Christians. Like most teachers, they believe if people had a better knowledge of the scriptures they would not have as many problems as they do!

Teacher Downside

Most teachers have difficulty acknowledging differing opinions. Teachers can hone their ability and benefit greatly by improving people and relational skills and developing greater sensitivity to their students.

Gifted teachers are greatly needed. They need to be reminded that their "students" actually eat truth like food, one bite and one plateful at a time!

Once I was on staff at a church where the pastor was a gifted teacher. At times he inundated us with so much information in a single lesson that we were on information overload! One day the pastor asked how he was doing and the youth pastor said, "Have you ever tried to drink water out of a fire hose?" He went on to explain that too much truth and information given too fast makes it impossible to actually retain it! If you can't ingest it then you can't digest it!

Teachers are a gift from God. If you are a teacher… then TEACH! The Body of Christ needs you to teach us the truth of God's word!

THE GIFT OF EXHORTATION

Read Acts 4:36, 11:23-26 and 14:22. Explain Barnabas' role in John Mark's life:

_____

_____

_____

_____

_____

"The gift of exhortation – sometimes called the gift of counseling – is the supernatural ability that God gives to certain members of the Body of Christ to minister words of comfort, consolation, encouragement and counsel to other members of the Body in such a way that they feel helped and healed."[4]

The Greek word, *ho-para-kalon* means, "to come alongside of (as in paraclete) Romans 12:8", but the literal meaning of the word is "a calling to one's own side", it is exercised by being able to share one's own confidence of God's provision and faithfulness and by providing encouragement.

The gift of exhortation can be used when preaching and teaching, or on a one-to-one basis.

Exhorter Character Qualities

Some people in the Body of Christ are motivationally gifted in the area of exhortation. I am one of them. I love to encourage people to live and walk victoriously in their Christian lives. Where teachers love for people to hear and learn the truth, exhorters love for people to DO the truth! Exhorters love a response to their message at the altar and to see transformation in people's lives. Their role includes encouraging, discipling, mentoring and training people to apply the truth. Exhorters tend to be equippers, usually very upbeat and positive, looking for the bright side to any situation.

Exhorter Downside

An exhorter won't stick around very long if counselees don't demonstrate real change. They are seen as giving too much advice or direction and tend to give methodical step-by-step directions to follow, even when advising a solution to an otherwise complex problem. Not every problem is cut and dried with a textbook solution.

One of my pastors once said, "How is my teaching on worship?" As an exhorter, I said, "Great, but when are we going to stop talking about it and DO it!"

We all can exhort others. Hebrews 3:13 – Some are specially gifted by the Holy Spirit to supernaturally exhort. Do it! Be a Barnabas! The Body of Christ needs you! Exhorters, exhort on!

THE GIFT OF GIVING

Read Mark 12:41-44. Explain the heart of this giver:

_____

_____

_____

_____

_____

"The gift of giving is a supernatural ability that God gives to certain members of the Body of Christ to joyfully and generously contribute their material resources above and beyond expected tithes and alms for the purpose of building Kingdom goals."[5]

The Greek word, *"ho-metadid-ous"* means, "sharing of material possessions" in Romans 12:8. This is not the giving of tithes and alms expected/required of all Christians (Luke 6:38).

C. Peter Wagner – "I am not ordinarily legalistic in my views of Christian behavior, but I believe anyone who is under the 10 percent figure *(of giving)* is engaging in a form of spiritual cheating. Some cheat the IRS regularly and get away with it. No one cheats God and gets away with it. 'Do not be deceived, God is not mocked; for whatever a man sows, that he will also reap.' (Galatians 6:7)."[6] *(my emphasis)*

R.G. LeTourneau was a Texan industrialist. He believed that the question is not how much of my money I give to God, but rather how much I keep. How much of his total percentage income did he give to God? _____

Read 2 Corinthians 8:1-2. What are the two ways the Macedonians gave?

_____

_____

_____

_____

_____

Read Acts 9:36-42. Explain how Dorcas gave.

_____

_____

_____

_____

Giver Character Qualities

Some in the Body of Christ are motivated to give. God's giving heart has been imparted to them. Thank God for the many givers who give of their resources, time and their all to Christ and His Body!

I have many friends who love to give generously to the Lord's work and His people. Gifted givers feel a part of the work they give to, seeing needs met. They often love to find projects, ministries or churches to reach people with the Gospel. They love to see results.

Givers are usually hard workers and have wisdom to see things through. They usually invest wisely and handle money well.

Giver Downside

Givers tend to be upset when others don't give as much as a giver thinks they should. Givers also need to be more involved in ministering, rather than just giving money. Family time and funds need to be closely guarded and regularly prioritized. It's too easy for a giver's loved ones to get kicked to the curb.

Motivations to Prompt Godly Giving:

- Focus on your love for God, not public attention. Matthew 6:1-4, *"Take heed that you do not do your charitable deeds before men, to be seen by them. Otherwise you have no reward from your Father in heaven. Therefore, when you do a charitable deed, do not sound a trumpet before you as the hypocrites do in the synagogues and in the streets, that they may have glory from men. Assuredly, I say to you, they have their reward. But when you do a charitable deed, do not let your left hand know what your right hand is doing, that your charitable deed may be in secret; and your Father who sees in secret will Himself reward you openly."*

- Desire earnestly to share with those in need. Ephesians 4:28, *"Let him who stole steal no longer, but rather let him labor, working with his hands what is good, that he may have something to give him who has need."*

- Sincerely love the one to whom you give. 1 Corinthians 13:3, *"And though I bestow all my goods to feed the poor, and though I give my body to be burned, but have not love, it profits me nothing."*

Attitudes of Godly Giving:

- Willing

- Extravagant

- Graceful

- Cheerful

- Joyful

- Simple (Romans 12:8)

- With integrity

- Hilarious (2 Corinthians 9:1-7)

THE GIFT OF ADMINSTRATION

Read Nehemiah 1-7. Explain Nehemiah's vision and determination:

_____
_____
_____
_____
_____

Read Judges 4-5. Explain Deborah's leadership aid.

_____
_____
_____
_____
_____

"The gift of administration is the supernatural ability that God gives to certain members of the Body of Christ to understand clearly the immediate and long-range goals of a particular unit of the Body and to devise and execute effective plans for the accomplishment of those goals."[7]

The Greek word, *"kubernesis"* means, "government or administration" in 1 Corinthians 12:28. Translated from the Greek it is *"helmsman."* The helmsman is in charge of getting a ship to its destination. The owner of the ship supplies the ship, hires the crew, chooses its business, etc. The helmsman or administrator is responsible to get it to its destination. The helmsman runs the everyday operations of speed, delegating tasks and completing the job.

A gifted administrator provides leadership, sees and takes care of functional tasks, organizes everything and everybody and keeps the main vision in the forefront.

Administrator Character Qualities

Some people in the Body of Christ are motivated by the gift of administration. They love everyday operations, delegation and completing the "job."

My wife, Terry, is not only motivated by serving but also by administration. I love watching her organize people and projects. I have often teased her that she could organize the Army! I remember once when Chuck Pierce came to our home for a meal. After observing her for about five minutes he said to Terry, "You cannot stand disorder, can you?" She said, "No, I cannot!"

Administrators love to set goals and objectives and put things in order. She loves working with leaders that have a clear vision. She can bring the details!

Terry is great at looking at the grand scheme of things and putting all the pieces together, much like someone who would take a model airplane and the directions and then proceed to systematically put it all together. Through the years, I have marveled at how she gets people to work together to complete a task. She makes work fun! She makes lists and knows how to change things, going over each event or task and debriefing others for suggestions to improve. Terry has led the Women's Ministry at Sonrise since it began and administrates meetings and events with excellence.

Administrator Downside

Gifted administrators tend to micromanage others, and not let go of delegates. They can be so task-focused that they forget about people. This makes them look like taskmasters! They can also become workaholics because they love their work so much.

Administrators are greatly needed in the Body of Christ to help leaders accurately steer to the ports of destination. They love to get a team to work together and celebrate victories together. You are a helmsman! If you have the gift of administration, then please! ADMINISTRATE!

THE GIFT OF MERCY

Read Luke 10:29-37. Who noticed the injured man? Who helped him?

_____

_____

_____

_____

_____

"The gift of mercy is the supernatural ability that God gives to certain members of the Body of Christ to feel genuine empathy and compassion for individuals, both Christian and non-Christian, who suffer distressing physical, mental or emotional problems, and to translate that compassion into cheerfully done deeds that reflect Christ's love and alleviate the suffering."[8]

The Greek word, _eleeo_ means, "to have compassion, pity, to have mercy on." All Christians should show mercy, but the life of those gifted in mercy revolves around doing good deeds of love toward others.

Giver of Mercy Character Qualities

People who are motivated by the gift of mercy have God's heart of mercy deposited into them. Over the years in ministry I have seen many men, women and young people who have the gift of mercy. Mercy givers are drawn to people who are in need and neglected. They have tendencies to sense people's hurts and needs. These people are heart-led rather than head-led. They love to pour God's love and mercy upon people.

Giver of Mercy Downside

Often mercy givers can cross the line of helping people and being big-time enablers. Tough love isn't easy for a mercy person. They need to guard against judging others who don't show mercy as they do. Every Christian needs to project the mercy of Jesus, but if you are supernaturally gifted in this area you will seek out the hurting. The Body of Christ and the world need you! If you are motivated by the gift of mercy, SHOW MERCY WITH WISDOM!

THE GIFT OF PROPHECY (PERCEPTION)

"The gift of prophecy is the supernatural ability that God gives to certain members of the Body of Christ to receive and communicate an immediate message of God to His people through a divinely anointed utterance."[9]

The Greek word, *propheteia* means, "the speaking forth of the mind and counsel of God."

It is important to be sensitive to the Holy Spirit. Perception or prophecy in the motivational category is a greater gift that we are to earnestly desire (1 Corinthians 14:1) and to covet (1 Corinthians 11:39). The word for desire and covet is *seloo* to strive for, to be eager, enthusiastically desirous or zealous for prophecy.

Prophecy is a "bubbling up" of the Holy Spirit within. It supernaturally flows or bubbles forth like a fountain. God is a God who speaks! God desires to be close and intimate with us and speaks directly through prophecy.

Prophecy declares the heartbeat of God to His Church for the purpose of edification.

Some people say preaching is prophecy. Prophecy is NOT preaching. We are to preach the Word, Jesus, the Christ and the Cross. (2 Timothy 4:2; Philippians 2:16; Acts 8:4, 15:35, 5:42; 1 Corinthians 1:23).

The gift of prophecy does not take the place of the written Word. Prophecy shall cease, but God's Word lives and abides forever.

Perceiver (Prophet) Character Qualities

Some people are gifted and motivated by the gift of prophecy. These people are motivated differently than others in the Body of Christ and they are often misunderstood.

Prophetically motivated people are very black and white people. They are sensitive to sin and the spirit realm. They are used by God to point out things we usually tend not to look at. Prophets declare the truth of God and His Word.

Perceivers Downside

Prophetically motivated people can be seen as condemning and rigid as well as negative vs. positive. Perceivers also tend to be off the charts self-analytical and can come across judgmental and intolerant of anyone who doesn't agree with them.

If you are a perceiver and motivated by prophecy, use your gift to help the Body of Christ! Remember to practice love when you dole out truth.

CHAPTER THREE
THE MINISTRY GIFTS

SO, YOU'RE CALLED TO LEAD US? Be humble, please!

Read Ephesians 4:7-13. List the ministry gifts and each purpose as a whole.

_____

_____

_____

_____

_____

_____

_____

_____

_____

_____

Often people have a unique mix of gifts, but each is an extension of the ministry of Jesus.

Ephesians 4:7, *"But to each one of us grace was given according to the measure of Christ's gift."*

THE GIFT OF APOSTLE

Read Romans 1:1. Clarify what Paul called himself and what he was called to:

_____

_____

_____

_____

"An apostle has a supernatural ability that is given by God to supernatural members of the Body of Christ enabling them to assume and to exercise general leadership over a number of churches, with an extraordinary authority in spiritual matters, spontaneously recognized and appreciated by those churches."[10]

The Greek word in noun or verb form, *apostello* means, "one sent forth."

Read Hebrews 2:4, Acts 19:11-12 and 2 Corinthians 12:12. What usually accompanies an apostle?

_____

_____

_____

_____

_____

Read Ephesians 2:19-22 and explain the "foundation."

_____

_____

_____

_____

_____

In Hebrews 3:1, who is the chief apostle?

_____

_____

_____

_____

_____

Read 1 Thessalonians 2:6 and Acts 15:22. Where does the authority of an apostle come from?

_____

_____

_____

_____

_____

Over whom do apostles exercise authority?

_____

_____

_____

_____

_____

Realities of Being an Apostle

Apostles plant churches.

An apostle is a wise master builder (1 Corinthians 2).

Apostles are last among Christians. 1 Corinthians 4:9-16, *"For I think that God has displayed us, the apostles, last, as men condemned to death; for we have been made a spectacle to the world, both to angels and to men. We are fools for Christ's sake, but you are wise in Christ! We are weak, but you are strong! You are distinguished, but we are dishonored! To the present hour we both hunger and thirst, and we are poorly clothed, and beaten, and homeless. And we labor, working with our own hands. Being reviled, we bless; being persecuted, we endure; being defamed, we entreat. We have been made as the filth of the world, the off scouring of all things until now. I do not write these things to shame you, but as my beloved children I warn you. For though you might have ten thousand instructors in Christ, yet you do not have many fathers; for in Christ Jesus I have begotten you through the gospel. Therefore I urge you, imitate me."*

Apostles provide vision, direction, planning, leading, creativity, ability to motivate, etc., comprehensive abilities given by the Holy Spirit to bless the Body of Christ.

Apostles are fathers, governors, judges of doctrinal issues and appointers who set elders and deacons into office.

Dr. David Cannistraci says, "The apostolic movement will consist of apostolic pacesetters who demonstrate power and lead apostolic people into apostolic positions all over the world."[11]

THE GIFT OF PROPHET

"The gift of prophet is a supernatural ability that God gives to certain members of the Body of Christ to receive and communicate an immediate message of God to His people through a divinely anointed utterance."[12]

Who is a Prophet?

- A prophet speaks forth or speaks for another.

- A seer – knowing the unknown

- A true prophet is open to correction.

- A prophet is to speak the truth and to be confirmed by the Body of Christ.

PROPHETS IN THE NEW TESTAMENT

First Prophet After John the Baptist

Acts 11:27-28, *"And in these days prophets came from Jerusalem to Antioch…"*

Prophets in the Church at Antioch

Acts 13:1-3, *"Now in the church that was at Antioch there were certain prophets and teachers: Barnabas, Simeon who called Niger, Lucius of Cyrene, Manaen who had been brought up with Herod the tetrarch, and Saul. As they ministered to the Lord and fasted, the Holy Spirit said…"*

Prophets Mentioned (1 Corinthians 12-14)

1 Corinthians 12:18, *"But now God has set the members, each one of them, in the body just as He pleased."*

1 Corinthians 14:29,32, *"Let two or three prophets speak, and let the others judge. And the spirits of the prophets are subject to the prophets."*

Prophetesses in the New Testament

- Acts 21:9 – Philip's four daughters

- Luke 2:36 – Anna the prophetess

The Purpose of a Prophet

- To confirm people in the Word of God – Acts 15:32, *"Now Judas and Silas, themselves being prophets also, exhorted and strengthened the brethren with many words."*

- To help build the foundation in the church of Christ – Ephesians 2:20, *"Having been built on the foundation of the apostles and prophets, Jesus Christ Himself being the chief cornerstone."*

- To bring revelation – Ephesians 3:5, *"Which in other ages was not made known to the sons of men, as it has now been revealed by the Spirit to His holy apostles and prophets."*

A Prophet's Character Qualities

- A prophet sees things as good or evil; black or white (Acts 5).

- The prophet tends to perceive or sense the character of a group (John 4).

- The prophet is usually bold and outspoken (Acts 21:10-14).

- The prophet is often given to brokenness (Isaiah 6:5).

- A prophet uses the principles of the Word of God as his base (Jeremiah 1:9).

- A prophet brings motivation, inspiration, illumination, confirmation, prioritization and persuasion.

Gift-Abuse, Misuse by a Prophet

- Correcting people who are not their responsibility

- Reinforcing a condemning spirit

- Judging and exposing an offender

- Dwelling on negative instead of positive

- Being severely self-judgmental

- Being intolerant of opinions of others if they disagree

THE GIFT OF EVANGELIST

"The gift of evangelist is a supernatural ability that God gives to certain members of the Body of Christ to share the gospel with unbelievers in such a way that men and women become Jesus' disciples and responsible members of the Body of Christ."[13]

Evangelists in the New Testament

Philip – Acts 21:8, "*On the next day we who were Paul's companions departed and came to Caesarea, and entered the house of Philip the evangelist, who was one of the seven, and stayed with him.*"

Timothy was Told to do the Work of an Evangelist (2 Timothy 4:5) By:

- Ordaining elders (Titus 1:5)

- Preaching the Gospel (Acts 14:21-28)

- Teaching the Word of God

- Establishing the believer

- Exhorting the believer

- Reporting to the home church

Jesus, the Evangelist

- John 4 – to one woman

- Matthew 4:23-25 – to the masses with signs and wonders

Doing the Work of the Evangelist

To Preach the Gospel

- In new places (Romans 15:20; 2 Corinthians 10:16)

- To all men (1 Corinthians 9:22)

- Without fear or embarrassment (Romans 1:16)

- Be constantly ready (Romans 1:15)

- In the face of opposition (Acts 13:45,50; Acts 14:2,5)

Teaching the Word

- Establishing the believer (Acts 14:21)

- Exhorting the believer (2 Timothy 4:2)

- Long-suffering with a new convert (1 Thessalonians 2)

Ordaining Elders (Acts 14:23)

Report to Your Home Church

- Work finished (Acts 14:26)

- Described what God had done (Acts 14:27)

- Supported the Mother Church (Acts 14:28)

- Out they go (Acts 15:36)

- To encourage and confirm

- To find out how they were doing

Evangelist Responsibilities are to be

- A soul-winner

- A church planter

- Bringing the Gospel of Jesus Christ to the lost

- Reaching out to the lost, meeting their needs

THE GIFT OF PASTOR

"The gift of pastor is a supernatural ability that God gives to certain members of the Body of Christ to assume a long-term personal responsibility for the spiritual welfare of a group of believers."[14]

The word "pastor" comes from the Greek word *poimen,* which means shepherd.

How a Pastor Functions (1 Peter 5:1-5)

- Shepherd

- Provider

- Caregiver

- Protector

- Guide

- Example

Responsibilities and Calling

- Appointed by the Holy Spirit

- Tends own vineyard (takes heed to self and family)

- Takes heed to all the flock

- Feeds the flock

- Points people to Christ

- Doesn't try to personally carry other people's burdens, so not to be crushed in the process

Jesus, our Chief Pastor (Shepherd)

- 1 Peter 2:25 (the shepherd and bishop over our souls) – *"For you were like sheep going astray, but have now returned to the Shepherd and Overseer of your souls."*

- Hebrews 13:20 – *"Now may the God of peace who brought up our Lord Jesus from the dead, that great Shepherd of the sheep, through the blood of the everlasting covenant."*

- 1 Peter 5:4 – *"And when the Chief Shepherd appears, you will receive the crown of glory that does not fade away."*

Timothy, a New Testament Example

- 1 Timothy 4:16 – *"Take heed to yourself and to the doctrine. Continue in them, for in doing this you will save both yourself and those who hear you."*

- Teach things that lead to godliness (v.11)

- Be an example (v.12)

- Read the Word, exhort, teach (v.13)

- Use your spiritual gifts (v.14)

- Meditate on the Word, be responsible, grow (v.15)

- Teach sound doctrine (v.16)

Warning to Pastors – Pray for Your Pastors!

- Ezekiel 34

- Feed the flock!

- Strengthen the diseased!

- Heal the sick!

- Bind up the broken!

- Bring back those driven away!

- Seek the lost!

The Church Today Needs Pastors for

- Covering

- Unity

- Care and feeding

- Counseling

THE GIFT OF TEACHER

"The gift of teacher is a supernatural ability that God gives to certain members of the Body of Christ to communicate information relevant to the health and ministry of the Body of Christ and its members in such a way that others will learn."[15]

- Teachers must give themselves to teaching (Romans 12:7).

- The teacher must know the Word of God (2 Timothy 3:16-17).

- All believers can teach, but not all have the gift of teaching (1 Corinthians 12:28-29).

Looking at Luke, Teacher Qualities Who Will

- Verify the truth (Luke 1:4)

- Base what is said on known truth (Luke 1:1-3)

- Be orderly in presentation (Luke 1:1-3)

- Research (Acts 1:1)

- Be accurate, and love accuracy (Luke 1:1-4; Ephesians 4:15-16)

- Seek out facts

- Be silent until information is gathered

The Body of Christ Needs Teachers to

- Teach sound doctrine

- Instruct

- Train

- Explain

- Nurture

- Be mature

- Lay out orderly teaching

- Be biblically oriented

- Be examples, *i.e.*, Pastor Carmont & Walter Martin

A Warning to Teachers

Read James 3:1 and state the warning.

_____

_____

_____

_____

The Gift of Teaching Can Be Used With

- Children

- Adults

- Masses

- Small groups

Super-natural Ability

- Communicate clearly

- Give effective application

- Provide the whole counsel of God

- Study and research

- Bring the known to the unknown

- Provide understandable illustrations

Greek for Teacher/Teaching

- *Didaskalia* "that which is taught"

- Ephesians 4:14 – content

- Romans 12:7 – teaching

- Romans 15:4 – learning (application)

- *Didache* "the act of teaching" (Titus 1:9)

- *Didaskalos* "the teacher" (Luke 2:46)

- *Didasko* "to give instruction" (1 Corinthians 4:17)

- *Didaktikos* "the ability to teach" (1 Timothy 3:2)

- *Didaktos* "the result of teaching" (John 6:45)

CHAPTER FOUR
MANIFESTATIONAL GIFTS

THEY DID, WHAT???

Manifestational gifts, the most dramatic of all the works of the Holy Spirit, are actually physical demonstrations of the reality of God's work. These gifts yield tangible, measurable evidence by way of supernatural manifestation. Each occurrence is supernatural and overtly reveals and punctuates the work of the Holy Spirit.

THE GIFT OF TONGUES

"The gift of tongues is a supernatural ability that God gives to certain members of the Body of Christ to receive an immediate message from God and communicate it to His people by way of a divinely anointed utterance – speaking audibly in an actual human or angelic language they have never learned."[16]

Defining Tongues

Tongues can be used in two ways – public and private. In both ways, tongues are Holy Spirit-inspired words for which the conscious mind plays no part.

Biblical References to Tongues

- Paul deals with tongues in Corinthians

- Luke deals with tongues in the book of Acts

- Tongues originate with the Spirit (Acts 2:4; 1 Corinthians 12:10, 14:2)

- *Latein glossa* – for speaking in tongues (Acts 10:45, 19:6; 1 Corinthians 12:14)

- May lead to accusations by unbelievers (Acts 2:5-8; 1 Corinthians 14:23)

- Is God-directed (Acts 2:11, 10:46; 1 Corinthians 14:2)

Get the Facts

1. Read Acts 2:2-4 and 1 Corinthians 12:14-26. Explain how there is both <u>unity</u> and <u>diversity</u> when speaking in tongues.

   _____

   _____

   _____

   _____

   _____

2. 1 Corinthians 13:8 states that tongues are temporary and will _____ .

3. The difference between prophecy and tongues found in Acts 19:6 and 1 Corinthians 12 is:

   _____

   _____

4. Read through the book of Acts. What was manifested _____ that was evidence revealing the Baptism of the Holy Spirit occurred?

5. We can use tongues to _____ ourselves (1 Corinthians 14:4; Jude 20).

6. In 1 Corinthians 14:14,15, we speak in tongues that our spirit might _____ .

7. Tongues are _____ by the Holy Spirit. This Divine utterance comes right through the lips of humans!

8. If tongues ARE accompanied by interpretation, they are equal to _____ (1 Corinthians 14:1-5,13,40).

9. ALL who speak in tongues publicly are directed to pray for _____ , as written in 1 Corinthians 14:13.

Tongues given by the Holy Spirit come from the depths of the human spirit.

Donald Gee – "The gift of tongues consisted of a power of more or less ecstatic speech, in languages with which the speaker was not naturally familiar."[17]

At the church of Corinth, the gifts were being exaggerated and misapplied. They spoke too much in tongues at their public meetings. This was confusing and out of order. Paul encouraged and taught balance by directing tongues to be accompanied with interpretation in an understood language.

The Purpose of Tongues

- Provide supernaturally-inspired communication to and from God – 1 Corinthians 14:2, *"For he who speaks in a tongue does not speak to men but to God, for no one understands him; however, in the spirit he speaks mysteries."*

- Edify the speaker, even if others aren't – 1 Corinthians 14:4, *"He who speaks in a tongue edifies himself, but he who prophesies edifies the church."*

- Bring edification to the Body of Christ

- Serve as a sign to the unbeliever – God can speak directly to someone in their own language, or the interpretation can speak to an unbeliever's heart – 1 Corinthians 14:22, *"Therefore tongues are for a sign, not to those who believe but to unbelievers; but prophesying is not for unbelievers but for those who believe."*

- Be used in private to pray and sing to God – 1 Corinthians 14:14-15, *"For if I pray in a tongue, my spirit prays, but my understanding is unfruitful. What is the conclusion then? I will pray with the spirit, and I will also pray with the understanding. I will sing with the spirit, and I will also sing with the understanding."*

- Be used when singing to God (1 Corinthians 14:15)

- Squelch pride of intellect and bring humility

Scriptural Checks and Balance

- Used at believers' meetings

- Differentiate between public and private tongues

- The gift needs to be facilitated by leadership

- Do not forbid speaking in tongues (1 Corinthians 14:39)

- It should edify

- Tongues will one day cease (1 Corinthians 13:8-10)

THE GIFT OF INTERPRETATION OF TONGUES

"The gift of interpretation of tongues is the supernatural ability that God gives to certain members of the Body of Christ to make known in the vernacular the message of one who speaks in tongues."[18]

It is a supernatural gift given to certain members of the Body of Christ to make known or interpret in understand-able terms the message God gave (through the one who spoke the tongue.) The interpretation does not stand alone as a gift by itself (1 Corinthians 12:10). It must always be associated with a tongue JUST spoken.

46

Inspired by God

Directly after a tongue is given in a language not understood, the interpretation is given in a language understood by the listeners – providing the dynamic equivalent of that which was spoken in tongues.

It is Interpretation Not Translation

Translation is a rendering from one language to another, word for word or term for term. Joseph interpreted the butler and baker's dreams. He did NOT translate them.

Interpretation may be shorter or longer than the tongue, itself.

Some say, "Men are speaking to God, not to me." Don't be narrow-minded!

What About Interpretation?

- It is supernatural, not a natural talent to translate

- It should be used in order (1 Corinthians 14:37-40)

- It is possible to feel in the Spirit the glow and uplift or burden of an utterance in an unknown tongue, but the purpose of the gift of interpretation is to make the understanding of the tongue available to all of its listeners.

- There is usually an immediate response by the interpreter to the utterance in tongues (1 Corinthians 14:27).

- Interpret one at a time

- There should only be two or three at the most in a meeting

- Faith is needed to interpret. Fear can stop it

- The gift of interpretation is mainly used during public worship. Speaking in tongues can be used in private, devotional speaking, prayer language or singing to God.

- Example of a Japanese girl who heard a person speaking in a prayer language saying, "You have tried Buddha, why don't you try Jesus?"

- Wait on this ministry

THE GIFT OF PROPHECY

The gift of prophecy is a gift of the Holy Spirit given to members of the body of Christ to edify, exhort or comfort believers.

The Three Reasons for Prophecy

Prophecy is intended to accomplish three things, as written in 1 Corinthians 14:3, *"But he who prophesies speaks edification and exhortation and comfort to men."*

- TO EDIFY – to build up the church – often it lifts a meeting into a heavenly, life-giving atmosphere. God speaks to a situation in the body to build it or an individual up.

- TO EXHORT – to call near, comfort, encourage and challenge.

- TO COMFORT – to console, to comfort during a trial or distress.

Prophecy is to be Tested

Test the content of each prophecy. Test whether the prophecy confirms or agrees with what God is already doing.

- Test the prophecy by determining its benefits.

- Test the prophet.

- Test the accuracy of the prophecy - does it come true?

1 Thessalonians 5:19-21, *"Do not quench the Spirit. Do not despise prophecies. Test all things; hold fast what is good."*

The one who prophesies is responsible for its use, misuse, suppression or control.

1 Corinthians 14:32, *"And the spirits of the prophets are subject to the prophets."*

Three Sources of Prophecy (good or evil)

1. The Holy Spirit – 2 Samuel 23:2, *"The Spirit of the LORD spoke by me, and His word was on my tongue."*

   Jeremiah 1:9, *"Then the LORD put forth His hand and touched my mouth, and the LORD said to me: 'Behold, I have put My words in your mouth.'"*

   Acts 19:6, *"And when Paul had laid hands on them, the Holy Spirit came upon them, and they spoke with tongues and prophesied."*

2. Evil or lying spirits – Isaiah 8:19-20, *"And when they say to you, "Seek those who are mediums and wizards, who whisper and mutter," should not a people seek their God? Should they seek the dead on behalf of the living? To the law and to the testimony! If they do not speak according to this word, it is because there is no light in them."*

   Matthew 8:29, *"And suddenly they cried out, saying, 'What have we to do with You, Jesus, You Son of God? Have You come here to torment us before the time?'"*

3. The human spirit – Jeremiah 23:17, *"They continually say to those who despise Me, 'The LORD has said, "You shall have peace"'; And to*

everyone who walks according to the dictates of his own heart, they say,
'No evil shall come upon you.'"

Ezekiel 13:2-3, *"Son of man, prophesy against the prophets of Israel*
who prophesy, and say to those who prophesy out of their own heart,
'Hear the word of the LORD!' Thus says the Lord God: 'Woe to the
foolish prophets, who follow their own spirit and have seen nothing!'"

Prophecy Serves as a Sign

Prophecy is a sign for the believer and the unbeliever. Read 1
Corinthians 14:22. Prophecy shows that God is present in the midst
of His people, thereby drawing the attention of the hearers toward
God.

Prophecy Discloses the Secrets of the Heart

Read 1 Corinthians 14:22-25. Prophecy manifests the secrets of the
heart of an unbeliever, and the "unlearned" or untrained get touched.
Possibly believers who "lack the gift" (Weymouth) or "ignorant
persons" (Wesley) begin to understand the truths and mysteries of
God!

The Enemy Loves to Silence True Prophecy

It's so easy to become formal. The enemy doesn't want the
supernatural power of God to be displayed.

Covet Prophecy! Ask for the Spirit and the Word

- If you have the Spirit without the Word, you'll blow up!

- If you have the Word without the Spirit, you'll dry up!

- If you have the Spirit and the Word, you'll grow up!

THE GIFT OF FAITH

"The gift of faith is a supernatural ability that God gives to certain members of the Body of Christ to discern with extraordinary confidence the will and purposes of God for the future of His work."[19]

Beliefs About Faith

- Some have said it seems as if a special faith comes into their hearts, a quickening

- Weymouth - "To a third man by means of the same Spirit, special faith."

- All Christians have faith.

It Seems as if There are a Number of Degrees or Shades of Faith (*pistis*).

First Degree – Faith can mean a body of truth, which we believe (Ephesians 4:13; 1 Timothy 6:20-21).

Second Degree – Faith can be the basic trust which one has in God for his/her salvation; or saving faith (John 3:15; Ephesians 2:8-9).

Third Degree – Faith can be loyalty, which is grown by the Holy Spirit of God (Galatians 5:22).

Fourth Degree – Faith can be a mountain-moving surge, which both Jesus and Paul speak about (Matthew 17:20, 21:21; 1 Corinthians 13:2).

Donald Gee – "It would seem to come upon certain of God's servants in times of special crisis or opportunity in such mighty power that they are lifted right out of the realm of even natural and ordinary faith in God and have a divine certainty put within their souls that triumphs over everything."[20]

51

We imitate our Father and speak those things that are NOT as though they were. Romans 4:17 – *"...He is our father in the sight of God, in whom he believed—the God who gives life to the dead and calls into being things that were not"* (NIV).

One man has said, "The gift of faith is the mysterious surge of confidence which sometimes arises within a person faced with a specific situation or need. It gives that person a trans-rational (otherly) certainty and assurance that God is about to act through a word or action. It is both the irresistible knowledge of God's intervention at a certain point and the authority to affect this intervention through the power of the Holy Spirit."

The gift of faith moves mountains! 1 Corinthians 13:2, *"And though I have the gift of prophecy, and understand all mysteries and all knowledge, and thought I have ALL FAITH, so that I could remove mountains, but have not love, I am nothing."* The gift of faith should always be used in LOVE!

It is easy if God has given you this gift to forget that others do not have the special impartation. Don't project it on others and discourage them! Encourage others by exercising YOUR gift in love!

Examples of the Gift of Faith

1 Kings 18:1-40 – Elijah at Mt. Carmel with the prophets of Baal.

Mark 11:12-26 – Have faith in God or the faith of God. Mountain-moving faith!

THE GIFT OF HEALING

Read 1 Corinthians 12:9. "The gift of healing is a supernatural ability that God gives to certain members of the Body of Christ to serve as human intermediaries through whom it pleases God to cure illness and restore health apart from the use of natural means."[21]

Healing Defined

The gift of healing is the actual event of healing itself, which a sick person receives. As there are many kinds of illnesses, so there are many different healing gifts. It is that event or progression which a person receives in the emotional, spiritual, or physical areas of life.

The Greek words for "healing" used in the New Testament are:

Therapeno - translated by the words "heal" and "cure." This is where the word "therapeutic" comes from.

Iaomai - always translated "heal" and "cure."

Faith Applied

One must have faith to operate in the gift of healing!

Not Just for the Sake of HEALING!

- Healing substantiates the claims of Jesus!

- Healing authorizes the Gospel message of God's servants.

- Healing shows Christ arose!

- Healing draws people to Christ.

The Example of Jesus

FATHER – Jesus only did what He saw the Father doing (John 5:17-21).

HOLY SPIRIT – Jesus healed through His relationship with the Holy Spirit (Luke 3:21-23, 4:1, 5:17).

HIS PRAYER LIFE – Forty days of prayer and fasting (Luke 4:1-13).

HIS PERSPECTIVE – Jesus healed the sick.

Four Gospels

JESUS HEALED because of His love and compassion. He spoke a word, He touched, He prayed, He fasted, He commanded, etc.

Spirit, Soul and Body

Healing is brought to all three parts of a human being. The healing of the SPIRIT is renewal and restoration of your spiritual life and relationship with God.

The healing of the SOUL is the healing of the mind, will and emotions. It grows out of pain/hurt from another person or time/experience in our past. Jesus heals the broken-hearted.

The healing of the BODY is healing applied to the physical (visible) part of our being (Matthew 9:35-38).

Show and Tell

- Jesus modeled His ministry – the twelve disciples and the Gospel.

- Jesus gave His ministry away (the Gospels).

- Jesus commanded them to go (Matthew 10:1-14).

- Jesus gave instruction (Matthew 8:1-14).

Minister Healing Biblically

- Healing miracles and gift of healing (Acts 4:12-16)

- The laying on of hands (Mark 16:15-18)

- Anoint with oil, pray in faith (James 5:13-16)

54

- Spoken Word and believing Word (Psalm 107:20)

- Pray the prayer of agreement (Matthew 18:19-20)

- Believe you receive when you pray (Mark 11:24-26)

- Partake of the Lord's Supper (1 Corinthians 11:26-32)

- Use the Name of Jesus (Mark 16:15-18)

*A Model of How to Pray for Healing

1. Interview

2. Diagnosis

   - Human knowledge

   - Supernatural knowledge

3. Prayer (according to the problem)

   - Natural causes

   - Sin causes

   - Could be command, pronouncement, intercession, petition, etc.

4. Pray for effect

   - Keep your eyes open

   - I agree with You, Lord

- Ask and observe if anything is happening

- We have to express what we want

5. Post-prayer instruction

- Go and sin no more

- Read a specific scripture

- As the Spirit leads - etc.

Taken from John Wimber's Healing Seminar notes[22]

Don't Be Confused

YOU CANNOT MANIPULATE GOD! One gifted or anointed to minister healing must be a mere vessel that God will use!

The energy or power of GOD is at work in and through the believer that brings healing.

Deliverance for the sick will destroy the works of the devil. Acts 10:38 – *"Jesus of Nazareth went about doing good and healing all that were oppressed of the devil."*

Healing attracts the attention of people to the Gospel of Christ in a way that will open their heart to the Good News!

Remember

- Jesus did only what He saw the Father do (John 5:17-21)

- Pray for people – keep praying

- Keep learning, that's what a disciple does/is

- Only Jesus has all the answers.

- Always minister in LOVE

THE GIFT OF WORKING OF MIRACLES

1 Corinthians 12:10, *"To another the working of miracles."*

"The gift of miracles is a supernatural ability that God gives to certain members of the Body of Christ to serve as human intermediaries through whom it pleases God to perform powerful acts that are perceived by observers to have altered the ordinary course of nature."[23]

Working of Miracles Defined

Miracle is a word often used to denote the non-natural, beyond-natural, supernatural or para-normal order of things.

The effects of miracles are events in which people are visibly and beneficially affected in an extraordinary way by the power of God working through an individual.

The word "working" in the Greek is *en-erg-ay-mah* – it means an effect, an operation, a working.

The word "miracles" is *dunamis* in the Greek. It means force, miraculous power, a miracle itself, worker of miracles, power, strength, etc. The word *dunamis* means "power." Dynamite!! It suggests the capacity of someone to carry out some event and it denotes a spontaneous expression of such "power." The central proof of God's power was the raising of Jesus from the dead. 1 Corinthians 6:14, *"And God both raised up the Lord and will also raise us up by His power."*

Miracles are sometimes called "powers," meaning explosions of the Almighty. "Wonders" means, staggering astonishment.

Working of Miracles

- Brings miraculous deliverance – Exodus 14:16, *"But lift up your rod, and stretch out your hand over the sea and divide it. And the children of Israel shall go on dry ground through the midst of the sea."*

- Confirms the Word of God – Acts 13:11-12, *"And now, indeed, the hand of the Lord is upon you, and you shall be blind, not seeing the sun for a time.' And immediately a dark mist fell on him, and he went around seeking someone to lead him by the hand. Then the proconsul believed, when he saw what had been done, being astonished at the teaching of the Lord."*

- Delivers people in danger

- Shows God's power and majesty

- Raises the dead!

- Points to King Jesus

Biblical Working of Miracles

The bringing of the shadow back ten degrees – Isaiah in 2 Kings 20:8-11, *"And Hezekiah said to Isaiah, 'What is the sign that the LORD will heal me, and that I shall go up to the house of the Lord the third day?' Then Isaiah said, 'This is the sign to you from the LORD, that the LORD will do the thing which He has spoken: shall the shadow go forward ten degrees or go backward ten degrees?' And Hezekiah answered, 'It is an easy thing for the shadow to go down ten degrees; no, but let the shadow go backward ten degrees.' So Isaiah the prophet cried out to the LORD, and He brought the shadow ten degrees backward, by which it had gone down on the sundial of Ahaz."*

Jesus in Mark 4:35-41 – The wind and the waves

Paul in Acts 19:11-12 – *"Now God worked unusual miracles by the hands of Paul, so that even handkerchiefs or aprons were brought from his body to the sick, and the diseases left them and the evil spirits went out of them."*

Peter in Acts 5:15 – *"So that they brought the sick out into the streets and laid them on beds and couches, that at least the shadow of Peter passing by might fall on some of them."*

Paul in Romans 15:18-19 – *"For I will not dare to speak of any of those things which Christ has not accomplished through me, in word and deed, to make the Gentiles obedient – in mighty signs and wonders, by the power of the Spirit of God, so that from Jerusalem and round about to Illyricum I have fully preached the gospel of Christ."*

Beware of False Miracles

There are false miracles! Revelation 16:14, *"For they are spirits of demons, performing signs, which go out to the kings of the earth and of the whole world, to gather them to the battle of that great day of God Almighty."*

Summing Up Miracles

The gift of miracles is closely associated with the gifts of an Apostle. 2 Corinthians 12:12, *"Truly the signs of an apostle were accomplished among you with all perseverance, in signs and wonders and mighty deeds."*

God works miracles without human intermediaries as well.

Hebrews 13:8, *"Jesus Christ is the same yesterday, today, and forever."*

It is a gift that is needed today. Be open to what the Lord might be doing.

THE GIFT OF THE WORD OF KNOWLEDGE

"A word of knowledge is a supernatural ability given to certain members of the Body of Christ to reveal a God-inspired utterance. The utterance is a supernatural insight into things *"freely given us by God,"* (1 Corinthians 2:12) divulging facts which the Holy Spirit wishes revealed. These facts are concerning a specific occasion or person with a practical application of an outpouring of God's love."[24]

Often a word of knowledge is used simultaneously with a word of wisdom. Wisdom is knowledge rightly applied.

Ephesians 1:17, *"That the God of our Lord Jesus Christ, the Father of glory, may give to you the spirit of wisdom and revelation in the knowledge of Him."*

The word of knowledge is seeing what God sees. The word of knowledge is NOT natural perception or knowledge. It is supernatural or extra-ordinary.

Hidden in the Lord are all the treasures of wisdom and knowledge. The Lord is omniscient, meaning all-knowing. A revelation springs forth by the Holy Spirit from the all-encompassing knowledge of God. This is a word of knowledge.

Word of Knowledge Illustrations

To Reveal Sin

- Nathan to David – 2 Samuel 12:1-7

- Elisha to Gehazi – 2 Kings 5:20-27

- Jesus to the woman at the well – John 4

- Peter to Ananias – Acts 5:1-6

To Help Find Something

- Samuel to Saul – 1 Samuel 9:15-20

- Samuel to Saul – 1 Samuel 10:22

To warn and provide safety

Elisha to the King of Israel – 2 Kings 6:8-23

To reveal thoughts

Jesus to the Scribes – Matthew 9:1-7

To provide healing

- Jesus to the paralytic – Matthew 9:1-7

- Jesus to the Roman official – John 4:45-54

To give insight to prayer

"A time to speak; a time to keep silent" – Ecclesiastes 3:7

Word of Knowledge Comes by

- Pictures

- Inner-knowing

- A picture of a written word

- Pain in the body

- A spontaneous utterance

- You "see it," "know it," "read it," "feel it" or "say it."

Word of Knowledge Summation

- For every ounce of the word of knowledge, a pound of wisdom is needed to apply it

- Be open to the Lord

- Pray

- Knowledge must be coupled with love

- Always in LOVE

- Love edifies

- Paul was given a thorn in his flesh because of revelation (2 Corinthians 12)

THE GIFT OF THE WORD OF WISDOM

"The word of wisdom is a supernatural ability given to certain members of the Body of Christ in an utterance inspired by God and spoken by an individual. It reveals part of the total wisdom of God. It is "seeing" what God sees in a situation and "saying" it. It is applying God's wisdom to a specific situation."[25]

Word of Wisdom Defined

The Greek word for "wisdom" is *sophia*. It is used by Paul 17 times in 1 Corinthians 1-3. The only other occurrence in 1 Corinthians is in 12:28 as *logos sophia*. It means wisdom (higher or lower, worldly or spiritual).

The root word *sophos* means "clear, wise" in a general application – wise.

Harold Horton – "The word of wisdom is therefore the supernatural revelation by the Spirit of Divine purpose; the supernatural declaration of the mind and will of God; the supernatural unfolding of the plans and purposes concerning things, places, people, individuals, communities, nations."[26]

It is the revelation of the purpose of God concerning people, things or events.

There is also godly wisdom that is NOT a word of wisdom.

Proverbs 9:10 – *"The fear of the LORD is the beginning of wisdom, and the knowledge of the Holy One is understanding."*

Proverbs 4:7 – *"Wisdom is the principal thing; therefore get wisdom. And in all your getting, get understanding."*

What the Word of Wisdom is NOT

- Deep spiritual insight into the Word

- A high degree of intelligence

- Administrative wisdom

- Simply being wise or having wise things to say

- Prudence, etc.

Word of Wisdom and How it is Used

- It is a divine flash of the light of God's wisdom. He is the only wise and all-wise God.

- It is used to warn of danger or harm

- It is used to reveal the future

- To give guidance or direction

- To reveal God's PLAN

Old Testament Illustrations

- Solomon (1 Kings 3:16-28). The result: They perceived his wisdom came from God.

- Joseph (Genesis 41:14-45). The result: Joseph is set in his place of authority. God is glorified!

- David and Nathan

New Testament Illustrations

- Jesus (Matthew 25:15-22). The result: marvelous!

- James (Acts 15:5-27). The result: agreement.

How the Word of Wisdom Comes

- NEEDED IN problem-solving situations

- NEEDED IN counseling

- NEEDED IN proclaiming of the Word of God

- Receiving a mind's eye picture

- Receiving a word of knowledge

- Receiving a prophetic utterance

Summing Up the Word of Wisdom

- The word of knowledge and wisdom often work together.

- Ounce of knowledge – pound of wisdom!

- Be open.

- Use the gift in LOVE.

Listen! Let God impart His wisdom to you!

THE GIFT OF THE DISCERNING OF SPIRITS

"The gift of discerning of spirits is a supernatural ability that God gives to certain members of the Body of Christ which enables them to know with assurance whether behavior purported to be of God is in reality divine, human or satanic."[27]

Discerning of Spirits Defined

- The Greek word is *diakrisis*, which means "judging through."

- Robinson - "distinguishing or discerning clearly"

- It's a piercing of the outward and seeing right through to the source.

- It is a supernatural perception into the spiritual realm for the purpose of determining the source of unseen spiritual activity.

Do Not Confuse

Don't confuse the gift of discerning of spirits with discernment which comes through experience.

Don't confuse discerning of spirits as a critical spirit in the natural. Some people see the wrong in everything or everybody. John Wesley said, "Such a "talent" might well be burned without grieving the Lord at all."

Hebrews 5:13-14, *"For everyone who partakes only of milk is unskilled in the word of righteousness, for he is a babe. But solid food belongs to those who are of full age, that is, those who by reason of use have their senses exercised to discern both good and evil."*

1 Corinthians 2:14-15, *"But the natural man does not receive the things of the Spirit of God, for they are foolishness to him; nor can he know them, because they are spiritually discerned. But he who is spiritual judges all things, yet he himself is rightly judged by no one."*

Like Prophecy, Three Possible Sources Are

- Spirit of God

- Human spirit

- Evil spirit

Gift of Discerning of Spirits is Used

- As a verbal gift

- During a disagreement between two parties

- During a conflict in ministry setting

- During demonic activity

- In a public or private setting

- When there is heaviness and unrest

- When there is uneasiness

By Contrast the Holy Spirit Brings

- Discernment, reveals motivating spirit or source

- Love

- Joy

- Peace

Ways Discerning of Spirits is Used

- To expose error

- Seducing spirits

- Lying spirits – 1 Timothy 4:1-2, *"Now the Spirit expressly says that in latter times some will depart from the faith, giving heed to deceiving spirits and doctrines of demons, speaking lies in hypocrisy, having their own conscience seared with a hot iron."*

- Doctrine of devils – 2 Peter 2:1, *"But there were also false prophets among the people, even as there will be false teachers among you, who will secretly bring in destructive heresies, even denying the Lord who bought them, and bring on themselves swift destruction."*

- Damnable heresies

To Expose a Servant of the Devil

Elymas the Sorcerer – Acts 13:9-10, *"Then Saul, who also is called Paul, filled with the Holy Spirit, looked intently at him and said, 'O full of all deceit and all fraud, you son of the devil, you enemy of all righteousness, will you not cease perverting the straight ways of the Lord?'"*

To Unmask Demonic Miracle Workers AND False Prophets

2 Thessalonians 2:9, *"The coming of the lawless one is according to the working of Satan, with all power, signs, and lying wonders."*

To Help the Church

Revelations 2:2,6, *"I know your works, your labor, your patience, and that you cannot bear those who are evil. And you have tested those who say they are apostles and are not, and have found them liars. But this you have, that you hate the deeds of the Nicolaitans, which I also hate."*

Revelations 2:14-15, *"But I have a few things against you, because you have there those who hold the doctrine of Balaam, who taught Balak to put a stumbling block before the children of Israel, to eat things sacrificed to idols, and to commit sexual immorality. Thus you also have those who hold the doctrine of the Nicolaitans, which things I hate."*

Revelations 2:20, *"Nevertheless I have a few things against you, because you allow that woman Jezebel, who calls herself a prophetess, to teach and seduce My servants to commit sexual immorality and eat things sacrificed to idols."*

CHAPTER FIVE
KNOW YOUR GIFT

GO FOR IT!

The gifts inside you have been deliberately designed and uniquely CREATED. You have been thoughtfully and strategically put here on this earth for a very specific reason! God thought of you and all your ways and characteristics, and *wanted* you to be who you are! He loves the way He made you and is a very proud Daddy!

Did you also know He planned your personality, the way you think, the way you behave, your strengths and even the areas where you are weak? You are a magnificent part of God's blueprint for the Body of Christ!

God intended for you to fit together with all the other gifts (people) in the church, to BE the Body of Christ! You need someone else's strengths, just like they need yours. Without you, there's not only something in the Body of Christ that is sorely missing, but with you the Body of Christ is one step closer to being exactly what God wants it to be.

Impartation

God wants the gifts of the Holy Spirit to be imparted to you!

Romans 1:11-12, *"For I long to see you, that I may impart to you some spiritual gift, so that you may be established – that is, that I may be encouraged together with you by the mutual faith both of you and me."*

One of the ways God has used me over the years has been to lay hands on people and begin to see spiritual gifts released through the laying on of hands. God wants to impart to you spiritual gifts. God wants to establish you!

Fear of failure can deform and cripple a person, ruining their self-esteem. This fear is also straight from the enemies of God. Failure promotes flawlessness like practice makes perfect. Making mistakes will teach you – if you let it. So, get on it! Grow, grow, GROW!!! Don't be afraid! We are all in this together. It's your chance to step up to the plate and hit the homerun of your life! GO for it! It's what you have been made for!

SOURCES

Fortune, Don & Katie, Discover Your God-Given Gifts, Fleming H. Revell Co., Chosen Books, Old Tommey, Tappan, NJ ©1987.

New King James Version (NKJV) ©1982 Thomas Nelson, Inc. Used by permission. All rights reserved.

HOLY BIBLE, NEW INTERNATIONAL VERSION ©1973, 1978, 1984 International Bible Society. Used by permission of Zondervan. All rights reserved.

---

[1] Wagner, C. Peter, Your Spiritual Gifts Can Help Your Church Grow, Ventura, CA, Regal Books © 2005. p. 33

[2] Strong, James, Strong's Exhaustive Concordance of the Bible, MacDonald Publishing Company, Mclean, VA.

[3] Wagner, C. Peter, Your Spiritual Gifts Can Help Your Church Grow, Ventura, CA, Regal Books © 2005. p. 126

[4] Ibid., p. 150

[5] Ibid., p. 93

[6] Ibid., p. 90

[7] Ibid., p. 152

[8] Ibid., p. 208

[9] Ibid., pp. 214-215

[10] Ibid., p. 192

[11] Cannistracti, David, The Gift of Apostle, Ventura, CA, Regal Books © 1996. p. 36

[12] Wagner, C. Peter, Your Spiritual Gifts Can Help Your Church Grow, Ventura, CA, Regal Books © 2005. pp. 214-215

[13] Ibid., p. 164

[14] Ibid., p. 141

[15] Ibid., p. 126

[16] Ibid., p. 219

[17] Gee, Donald, Concerning Spiritual Gifts, Springfield, MO, Gospel Publishing House © 1975.

[18] Wagner, C. Peter, Your Spiritual Gifts Can Help Your Church Grow, Ventura, CA, Regal Books © 2005. p. 222

[19] Ibid., p. 153

[20] Gee, Donald, Concerning Spiritual Gifts, Springfield, MO, Gospel Publishing House © 1975.

[21] Wagner, C. Peter, Your Spiritual Gifts Can Help Your Church Grow, Ventura, CA, Regal Books © 2005. pp. 225-226

[22] Wimber, John, Healing Seminar Notes, Vineyard Ministries International.

[23] Wagner, C. Peter, Your Spiritual Gifts Can Help Your Church Grow, Ventura, CA, Regal Books © 2005. p. 224

[24] Ibid., p. 203

[25] Ibid., p. 206

[26] Horton, Harold, The Gifts of the Spirit, Springfield, MO, Gospel Publishing House © 1975. p. 56

[27] Wagner, C. Peter, Your Spiritual Gifts Can Help Your Church Grow, Ventura, CA, Regal Books © 2005. p. 99